# Meditations to Make Teachers Smile

# Meditations to Make Teachers

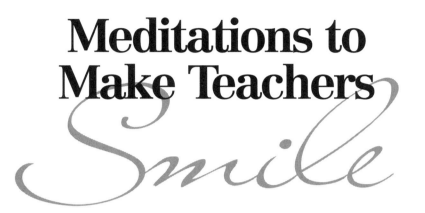

## Lisa Flinn

## Illustrated by John McPherson

**DIMENSIONS**
FOR LIVING
NASHVILLE

MEDITATIONS TO MAKE TEACHERS SMILE

*Copyright © 2001 by Dimensions for Living*

*This book is printed on acid-free paper.*

**Library of Congress Cataloging-in-Publication Data**

Flinn, Lisa, 1951–
  Meditations to make teachers smile / Lisa Flinn; illustrated by
John McPherson.
    p. cm.
  ISBN 0-687-07368-5 (alk. paper)
    1. Teachers—Prayer-books and devotions—English.   2. Education
(Christian theology)—Meditations.   I. Title.
BV4596.T43 F58 2001
242'.68—dc21                                                         00-050896

Scripture quotations are from the New Revised Standard Version of
the Bible, copyright © 1989, by the Division of Christian Education
of the National Council of the Churches of Christ in the United
States of America. Used by permission.

01 02 03 04 05 06 07 08 09 10 —10 9 8 7 6 5 4 3 2 1

MANUFACTURED IN THE UNITED STATES OF AMERICA

To the wonderful teachers
of Orange County Schools, North Carolina,
and to one of the finest students I know,
my daughter Louise Flinn

*F*ollowing his last language arts class, Mr. Jones headed to the gym to coach the girls' basketball team.

*"Hey, Coach!" called a player. "Will you blow up this ball?"*

*The coach attached the air hose to the ball's valve and allowed the air pressure to build . . . and build . . . and build. . . .*

*Backing away in fright, the girl shouted, "Stop, Coach! It's going to explode!"*

*While releasing some of the air pressure, the coach replied, "Oh, didn't you ask me to blow up the ball?"*

*"Uh, yeah," she choked.*

*"Next time you should say 'inflate.' "*

Remember the adage "Say what you mean and mean what you say"? It's an apt lesson for students, but it applies to teachers as well. Most of us have been known to send mixed messages, be vague, or even stray into hypocrisy. And who catches us in the act? Our students! With their amazing ability to find our faults, they are God's missionaries for truth and clarity, sent to keep us on our toes.

> **Listening Lord, help me to choose my words wisely.**

*O*n Monday morning Ms. Hunley's students arrived to find the classroom walls newly decorated with vivid posters from around the world.

*The teacher explained, "America is a country of immigrants. All of us have a history that goes back to another country, unless you are a Native American."*

*"Why do we have to learn about all that stuff?" complained one boy.*

*"Don't you want to know about your forefathers?" she asked.*

*"You must be crazy, Ms. H," he replied. "I don't have four fathers."*

We research, plan, requisition, and craft; yet when we're ready to present our dynamic lesson, we're faced with apathy or even resistance. God has had a similar experience with some of us. After having inspired a great textbook for living, sent a really miraculous teacher, and created a divine Spirit to help us with our "homework," God is still faced with a lot of lackluster students.

---

**Sometimes my Bible is dusty, my church attendance is irregular, and I know I'm not practicing my faith as I should. Forgive my apathy, Lord. I will do better—with your help.**

---

*D*uring August, the faculty bulletin board filled rapidly with notices, calendars, and sign-up sheets. Searching for a spot to pin up another item, the department chair was met with a warning of sorts. Posted on red construction paper in the center of the board was the day's cryptic crossword puzzle from the newspaper. It read: "Committee work is like a soft chair: easy to get into, but hard to get out of."

Too often a sense of duty or the desire to please our superiors lands us in a "soft chair," involving us in work that does not suit the strengths and talents God has bestowed on us. God does not expect us to be good at everything or to serve in every capacity. As 1 Corinthians 12:7 tells us, each of us is given a manifestation of the Spirit to discover and use for the common good and for our own good.

> **Guide me, Lord, toward the best use of my time and talents, so that I may serve wisely and well.**

*M*s. Bennington began her first year of teaching with classic enthusiasm for her new profession. Following an energetic day of teaching, she also provided after-school tutoring. She began to worry about one student who was struggling with high school English. Despite the student's extra efforts, Ms. Bennington was disappointed to see that he had made a D on his exam. Her sympathy prompted her to scrawl "sorry" next to his grade. Upon receiving his graded exam, the young man moaned, "You're right, Ms. B, this was pretty sorry."

The passing of years and hundreds of students inevitably brings some disappointments. Little by little these setbacks and sorrows can harden our hearts. Just as we trust that God will be compassionate with us, despite our sorry behavior, may our students also trust us to keep our hearts open to them when they are in need of some understanding and mercy.

> Today, Lord, help me to be as merciful and tenderhearted to my students as you are with me.

*L* ouise was dressed to play a part in a class video project. Wearing an authentic Victorian costume, she walked up and down the halls and out on the school grounds while the taping was underway. As she passed the school's monitoring teachers, vice principals, and police officer, they smiled and nodded. No one asked her for a pass or an explanation.

*After changing into her regular clothes and heading back to class, Louise immediately was converged upon by the authorities.*

*"Do you have a pass?"*

*"Where are you going?"*

*"Why aren't you in class?"*

*"Who do you think you are, missy?"*

*Abashed, Louise replied, "I'm the same girl who was wearing the Victorian dress. Don't you recognize me?"*

Most of us make judgments about others based on their appearance. We're even critical of ourselves. Sometimes we really want to be noticed (particularly when we're looking good), while other times we hope no one sees us as we dash into the store in our ratty old sweats.

Thankfully, God recognizes us and loves us no matter how we're dressed, for mortals "look on the outward appearance, but the LORD looks on the heart" (1 Samuel 16:7).

Forgive me, Lord, for my hasty and misguided judgment of others. Help me to have the patience and wisdom to see people as they truly are.

*While monitoring the agricultural wing during the first week of school, a teacher spotted a bewildered freshman who was close to being trampled by a stampede of students. With lightning speed, the "ag" teacher twirled his rope and lassoed the stray girl.*

*As he gently pulled her away from the herd of students, he said, "Howdy, Ma'am. Can I help you get to where you're going?"*

*Staring down at the teacher's cowboy boots, she blurted, "Oh my gosh. I'm really lost. I thought this was Clark City High School."*

If you ever were lost as a child, you know the spasm of fear that first gripped you, followed by the wave of relief that washed over you when you were found. As adults, we, too, can become "lost." Problems with our health, a relationship, or a work situation can evoke a similar feeling of fear. In such times, our faith is the compass that will guide us from unfamiliar ground to peace.

**Be my landmark, O God, when I am "lost."**

*A*fter handing back the graded papers, the teacher heard a gasp and a giggle. "What's going on?" he asked.

*"Johnny said the F word," announced a gleeful girl. "I want to speak with both of you," responded the teacher.*

*When the three were huddled around the teacher's desk, the tattler whispered, "Johnny said he failed."*

Novelist Allan Gurganus has said that "in America, the true *F* word is *failure*." From the classroom to the boardroom, *failure* does seem to be a "dirty word." But failure is sometimes necessary in order to bring about change. It is through our failures that God teaches us to perceive life afresh, to mend our stubborn ways, and to discover a new course of action.

> God, I want to help my students see that their failures do not have to be bad endings; they can be opportunities for good beginnings.

*O*n a spring-cleaning rampage, the computer teacher came across a box of clothes from her college days. Fingering the lime green halter top and the brown-and-orange sweater dress, she reasoned she no longer had the youth or the figure to wear these fashions. She closed the lid and delivered the box to the thrift shop, not realizing that several photos were still inside.

*After spring break, she was taken aback to see two students dressed in her vintage 1970s garb.*

*"Ms. G," they giggled, "thanks for these great clothes! Who knew you were so cool?"*

*With trepidation, she asked, "How did you know those clothes were mine?"*

*"Oh, uh, you know," they stammered, "stuck in a pocket were some photos of you burning your bra."*

No matter how "cool" or embarrassing our youthful follies may have been, we must own them, for they are a cornerstone of who we are today. The choices we made, the challenges we met, and perhaps even the trouble we got into somehow led each of us to the decision to become a teacher. Therefore, should evidence of our colorful pasts arise, we shouldn't run or hide. Instead, we can stand firm and quote the apostle Paul: "When I was a child, I spoke like a child, I thought like a child, I reasoned like a child; when I became an adult, I put an end to childish ways" (1 Corinthians 13:11).

> **Lord, despite the foibles of my youth, I want to be a good adult role model for my students. Keep me ever mindful that my actions reflect not only on me, but also on the teaching profession.**

*O*ne afternoon, a visiting professor from a for-
eign country enrolled his daughter, Kwan, in
the third grade. After giving her a classroom
orientation, the teacher explained that a field trip
was scheduled for tomorrow and that Kwan would
need to bring a lunch. Eagerly, Kwan begged her smil-
ing father to let her make a real American sandwich.
With welcoming hospitality, the teacher offered to
accompany them to the grocery store after school and
help them select many sandwich ingredients.

The next day, Kwan proudly offered her new
teacher the first bite of a peanut butter, jelly, mayon-
naise, bologna, pickle, cheese, and tomato sandwich.

"This is a most American sandwich!" the teacher
exclaimed before gingerly taking a bite.

A pregnant teen, a bullied middle-schooler, or a
dyslexic second-grader are among many students who
feel like foreigners in their own schools. Despite the
demands on our time, we must find a way to show
hospitality to these students. By sharing a sandwich
or a personal story, we may help them feel less like
strangers and more hopeful about their lives.

> Lord, your Word tells us that by showing hospitality
> to strangers, we may entertain angels without
> knowing it (Hebrews 13:2). I shall do my best.

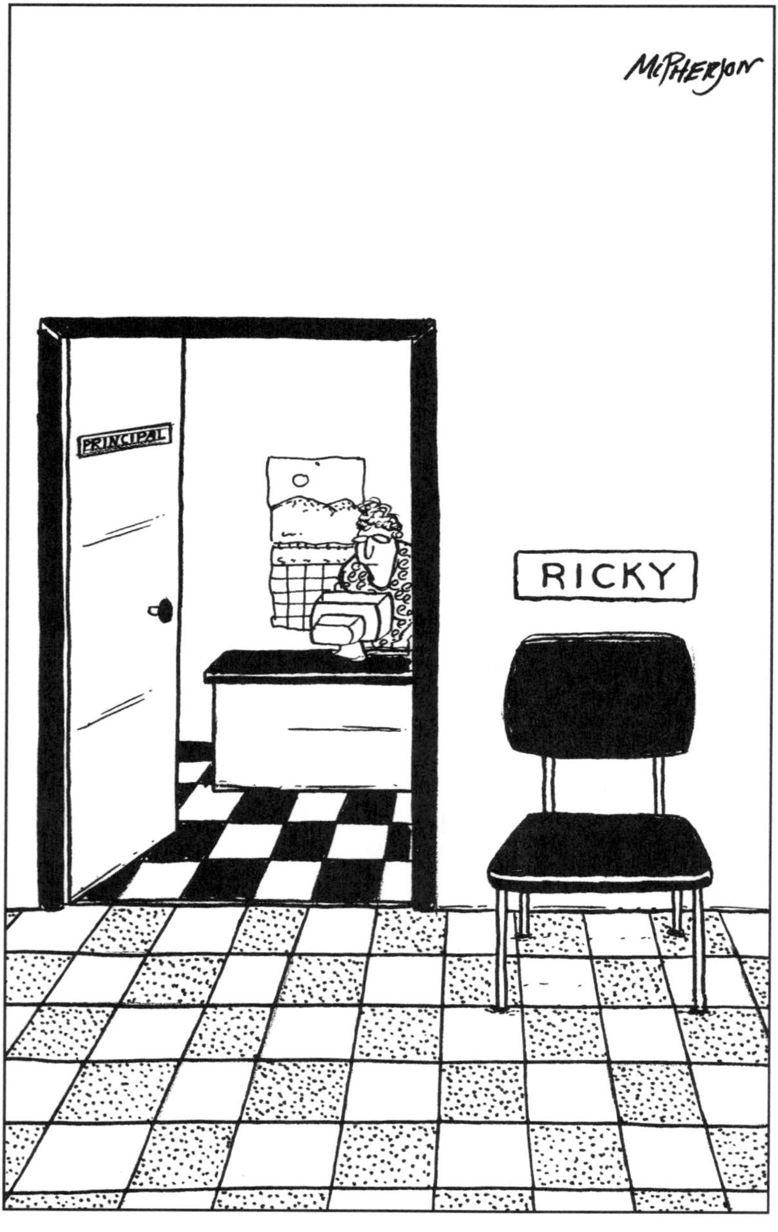
McPHERSON
PRINCIPAL
RICKY

*R*icky was in trouble so often that he had a personal chair outside the principal's office. The frustrated principal had tried every approach he could think of to put the wayward boy on the right path.

"It's too bad this school no longer has corporal punishment," grumbled the principal one day when Ricky was sent to the office again.

"Gee, I didn't know this place used to be a military school," Ricky replied.

We work to guide our students onto the right paths by improving their behavior, building their intellect, and nurturing their spirits. Year by year and grade by grade, we lead them toward graduation and a promising future as adults. May God inspire in us the wisdom, love, and courage to meet the challenge of our profession.

> **Teach me your ways, O Lord, and lead me on the right paths.**

*M*ommy, tell me a story," begged the kinder-gartner at bedtime.

"As you wish," granted the child's profes-sor mom as she began reciting the Canterbury Tales in Middle English.

After a moment of wonder followed by frustration, the child cried, "Mommy! Stop talking in cursive!"

When we pray at night, does God sometimes wonder if we are "talking in cursive"? Even within the privacy of prayer we can find it hard to speak honestly about our motivations, our problems, our fears, and our needs. Perhaps we are so accustomed to explaining, blaming, justifying, and defending ourselves to the world at large that we have trouble talking to our Maker. But we must try, for if we speak from the heart, God will understand our every word.

> **Lord, I do not know how to pray as I ought, but I will try to be more trusting and open in my conversations with you.**

*C*hristopher, a precocious kindergartner, was curious about every aspect of the school experience. During his first week of riding the school bus, he overheard two worried kids discussing a very tricky true-or-false test they had just taken.

*"You never know what kind of test they'll surprise you with next," fretted one boy.*

*The next morning, a substitute bus arrived to pick Christopher up. Confused, he tried to think of all he had learned about school thus far. Then it hit him: this was a test! Backing away from the yawning yellow doors, Christopher shouted, "It's a false bus!"*

With ever increasing emphasis on testing and accountability, we feel as if we're being tested as surely as our students are. Every year the standards are higher, and our stress levels rise along with them. No wonder we worry; but while we're worrying, fretting, and obsessing, we're losing precious time and energy. A wise teacher once said, "Can any of you by worrying add a single hour to your span of life?" (Matthew 6:27). Of course not; so try not to worry. Teach happy.

> **Dear God, help me not to worry about tomorrow but, instead, to make the most of this day.**

*A* student teacher had been placed at a preschool for the hearing impaired. One day during naptime, he noticed a child, curled up on her cot, signing to the wall.

"What's she doing?" the novice inquired of another child.

"She's talking to her imaginary friend."

Creativity is among the brightest blessings from God. So integral is it to our very nature that our lives would not be the same without it. May we not take this gift for granted but employ it, develop it, and celebrate it every day—at school and at home.

> Heavenly Creator, thank you for the richness and pleasure that life holds for us because you have shared the gift of creativity.

*S*everal Sunday school teachers had been working on a play about Noah and his ark. The cast
was largely composed of pairs of animals, with
the speaking parts going to God, Noah, and Noah's
sons. The audience sat in the fellowship hall facing
the door to the kitchen. The wall surrounding the door
was covered and painted to resemble the ark. Noah
called the wandering "animals," and they obediently
boarded the ark two by two. Then Noah called his
sons and their wives. Moving quickly, they boarded
the ark, shut the door, and locked it, leaving a surprised Noah standing outside alone.
From inside the ark came a muffled cry: "Mutiny!"

It's one thing to choose to be alone and quite another to be left out. Whether you're a toddler or an adult,
it brings an unhappy feeling. Because children lack
subtlety, we can look around any playground and see
who's being excluded. As adults, we are more clever
than our young students, so we try not to "hurt others' feelings" when we exclude them; yet we are often
not as clever as we think we are, and those who are
left out usually know it.

This week let's allow the Holy Spirit to lead us
toward including, not excluding.

> **Lord, forgive my selfishness and help me
> to remember the golden rule.**

McPHERSON

*A*s she led the class out to the playground, Ms. Lightfoot saw a double rainbow shimmering in the sky.

*"Class, look at the rainbow!" she called excitedly.*

*All the children but one rushed out to gaze in wonder.*

*"Tommy, come see!" they shouted to a reluctant classmate.*

*"No," Tommy said. "If we look, I know she'll make us write a poem about it."*

Sometimes we are as reluctant as Tommy when it comes to appreciating the beauty that surrounds us and thanking God for it. As we rush off to work, do we delight in the fresh morning breeze or listen to the beautiful birdsong? After we're home, do we take a moment to revel in the colors of the sunset? Don't forget that the sights, sounds, aromas, and textures of creation can calm, revitalize, and balance our weary selves.

Right now, take a moment to step outside and enjoy the extravagant blessings of nature.

---

**Thank you, God, for the beauty of the earth, which is always there to soothe my soul.**

*T*he first meeting of the German club had a rather meager attendance; and when the second meeting came to order, the number had dwindled even further. The club president, who had grand plans for the coming year, was beginning to feel desperate. Thinking quickly, he gave a rousing speech and then led a march down the hall, whereupon the German club annexed the French club.

Haven't we all felt a little desperate when we've thought that our plans were falling apart? It seems that the more things crumble, the more control we seek to exert.

As difficult as it is, we must sometimes accept that our wonderful plans are a complete mess. When we realize the Holy Spirit may be trying to work in our lives, we will benefit more than we can know.

> **All-knowing God, give me the trust to let go of plans when they're not working, so that I may be open to new possibilities.**

*F*ollowing the funeral of a well-known church member, a Sunday school teacher was questioned by one of her students.

"Did anyone call heaven and make a reservation for Mr. Smith?" the small boy asked.

"Oh, Mr. Smith doesn't need a reservation. God welcomes all believers into heaven."

"I'm not so sure," he worried aloud. "Jesus was God's only son, and he needed a reservation."

"Why do you say that?" inquired the puzzled teacher.

"Well, in Sunday school you told us that after Jesus died, he had to wait three days for the reservation of his body."

There are so many hard concepts to teach in Sunday school. The task is made easier, however, because children usually listen to and accept the lessons with great trust and belief. The faith of children is beautiful and enviable; when they are offered genuine knowledge and understanding of the Word, they respond with the desire to grow in faith.

**All-knowing God, make of me a worthy teacher.**

*Mrs. Younger, the new school librarian, was experiencing some discipline problems with an unruly class of fourth graders. The week before, the group had surreptitiously thrown spitballs, which she later found encrusting the bookcases, the carpet, and the brand new chairs. She hoped to put an end to their latest antics by reading the famous spitball chapter from* Otis Spofford, *because Otis gets his comeuppance. Mrs. Younger thought the kids would get the message. As she read, the class seemed to be listening, even behaving. Relieved, the librarian closed the book, looked up, and was met with a hailstorm of spitballs.*

Every teacher has a bad day now and then; it's to be expected. But what do we do if we're having a bad *year*? When every day is a struggle, we can become quite discouraged. The advice of colleagues and the support of family and friends are helpful; but if we seek sustained strength and lasting hope, we must turn to God for the personal power we need.

> **God, I ask for the assurance that things will get better. Stand by me as I face each day.**

*Mrs. Newton and the art club were working after school on a large mural for the cafeteria. On the tables were paper cups brimming with brightly colored paints, as well as a few cups of soda for the thirsty artists. Enjoying themselves immensely, the group joked, spilled, laughed, and painted.*

*"Time to finish up," declared the happy but exhausted teacher. "I'm tired and I'm starving!"*

*As she reached absently for her soda, she mistakenly took a sip of lime green paint.*

*"Yuck!" she cried between green lips and teeth.*

*"Oh, she's just like Van Gogh," said one student dryly. "She's so hungry she even eats her paint."*

Isn't it great that God gives us laughter along with the labor of teaching? The crazy mistakes, the tangled tongue bloopers, the inside jokes, and the silly surprises are the comic relief we all need to save our sanity. Every day, give yourself a reason to smile.

> **Thank you, Lord, for the pleasure of smiles and the joy of laughter. I'll take them with me wherever I go.**

*T*he well-dressed young man approached the house, briefcase in hand. He rang the doorbell and waited. Momentarily, a woman answered the door.

*Spying his briefcase, she said, "I don't wish to be surveyed, preached to, or sold anything."*

*She quickly closed the door, so the man rang again.*

*"I said I'm not interested," snapped the woman.*

*For a third time, the persistent man pressed the bell. Curious about the commotion, the woman's son came bounding to the door.*

*"Go away!" the frustrated mother shouted.*

*"Mom!" the boy shrieked in horror. "That man is my teacher!"*

We're not always a welcome sight, are we? It's no secret that parents and teachers can be at odds with each other. Both want what's best for the child. The parents have the experience of years with their child, whereas the teacher has a perspective gained by working with many children over time.

In conflicts with parents, we should heed the Bible story about the two women who each fought to claim a baby as her own (1 Kings 3:16-28). True loving concern must prevent us from "tearing a child apart" with our differences.

> **O Wise One, let my words be gracious, my intent pure, and my reasoning clear as I talk with parents.**

*W**here is Estonia?"*
*"What happened to your shirt?"*
*"When is the report due?"*
*"Why do we call this a 'hypotenuse leg'?"*
*"When did you want that report?"*
*"Who was the shortest president?"*
*"When did you say you wanted that report again?"*
*"How do we know that's true?"*
*"Is that your* real *hair?"*

Questions, questions, questions! All day long, from the insane to the interesting, we field many questions. Some bring us joy and deserve our time. Others make us exercise every ounce of restraint we have. It's a challenge to be patient, but we have to try.

Remember, even young Jesus asked his teachers a lot of questions (Luke 2:46).

---

**Lord, I wish I knew the right way to answer each question, but I don't. Help me to respond with patience and with wisdom.**

*Near the end of a grueling week, the honors students begged their teacher, Ms. D'Annunzio, to excuse them from their weekly exam.*

*"Such a gifted group of students should be quite capable of taking the test on Friday," she responded.*

*"Aw, come on, Ms. D!" they whined. "You know we've had a terrible week."*

*"Well . . . I'll cancel your test only if you present me with a hecatomb," she said cryptically.*

*Upon entering her room the next day, she was greeted by twenty-five robed students chanting an incantation. With a flourish, one student poured a clear liquid over the contents of a brass bowl and struck a match. Flames shot upward. Ms. D'Annunzio stepped forward to see the fire consuming one hundred gummy cows.*

*"A hecatomb," she marveled, as the smoke detector began to shrill.*

The moral: Teachers, be careful what you ask for! With flashes of brilliance and moments of sheer mischief, our students can surprise us.

God can surprise us, too, by answering our prayers in ways we'd never expect. With love and wisdom, God prevails over our requests, bringing lessons, gifts, and guidance in divine time and ways.

**Our Father, who is in heaven, hallowed is your name. Your kingdom come, your will be done, on earth as it is in heaven.**

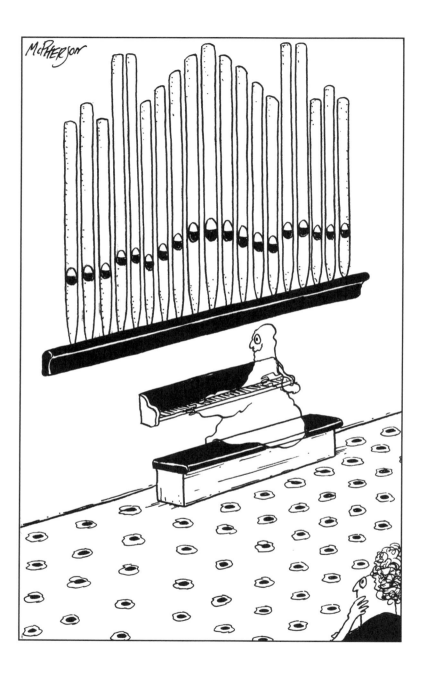

*T*wo Sunday school teachers, the organ repair-
man, the minister, a custodian, and a choir
member all said they had seen a ghost at the
old church within the past six weeks. Several concerned teachers were discussing whether to hold the
annual elementary sleepover at church.

Overhearing their conversation, Mrs. Barnhill's
young son piped in, "Mom, we'll be okay at church.
The Holy Ghost is there to protect us."

Going to church, tithing regularly, and living as God
has commanded does not guarantee our safety in this
world. Human imperfection causes bad things to hap-
pen, even in churches and schools.

We cannot stand against evil if we are mere ghosts
in our belief. Our faith in goodness and in God must
shine brightly in the darkness, so that the darkness
will not overcome our world.

> **O God, I will let my light shine as I love you
> with all my heart, soul, and might.**

*After the holiday, the elementary school's Spanish teacher was hoping to review the names of fruits with her students.*

*She held up an orange, asking, "What is this?" No one answered.*

*Next she showed the students an apple. "What is this?" she questioned, but no one spoke.*

*Holding up a banana, she tried again. "What is this?"*

*After a period of silence, one boy responded, "Well, if you're the teacher and you can't remember the answers, how do you expect us to remember?"*

A recent study found that people who are competent in their work recognize that they could improve on their performance. Conversely, people who are incompetent think they are doing a really great job.

Of course, we need a certain amount of confidence in order to control our students and teach our lessons, but some humility creates a good balance. Even within the walls of our classrooms, we are not all-knowing, all-wise, or all-powerful; only God is. If we don't acknowledge this, someone will be sure to point it out.

> **Almighty God, may my pride never keep me from improvement.**

*I*n the school's greenhouses, Mr. Thomas was experimenting with a new tomato hybrid. For many weeks he fussed over the cherry tomatoes. *Ever protective of his plants, the teacher warned everyone not to touch the ripening fruit.*

*When the long-awaited day finally arrived, Mr. Thomas rushed in to find that the bright red tomatoes were gone. Angrily he called his class together, saying, "Those experimental tomatoes have been eaten by someone. They were genetically altered plants, so I just don't know how that person will feel after eating them."*

*He hoped the person would feel guilty—and maybe even a little worried. But he didn't expect to get a call from the hospital. The voice on the other end of the phone said, "We've been requested to pump a student's stomach. Will you tell us about your experimental tomatoes?"*

Anger caused Mr. Thomas to be a little vengeful, which he later came to regret. In his guilt and embarrassment, he kept thinking, "Vengeance is mine . . . says the Lord" (Romans 12:19).

We are only human, and we occasionally will lose our temper. When our blood pressure rises, may we not seek vengeance, for we will reap what we sow.

> **Lord, forgive me for the things
> I have said in anger.**

*I*n May, the first-grade teacher invited her class to a picnic at her home.

Staring at the invitation, one girl remarked, "Mrs. McIver, I thought you said you live at school."

Arriving early to prepare, teaching all day, staying late for meetings, tutoring or coaching, and then returning for an evening program or game does make us feel like we live at school. We dedicate long hours, devote our hearts to our students, and always strive to improve each lesson because teaching is not only our work but also our mission.

Jesus is our inspiration. He reached out in love to all who needed him—even on the Sabbath—offering lessons that have transcended the ages. Like us, Jesus was a teacher. He understands what it means to "live" your work.

> **Lord, keep my heart and my mind steadfast and true. Give my body the strength to see me through.**

*A*s he pulled the returned books from the collection bin, the librarian noticed a rather fishy smell. Expecting to find a real fish, thrown into the bin as a prank, he carefully withdrew each book from the pile. There was no fish, but the odor remained. One by one, he picked up each book and sniffed it. Finally, he found the offending one. Checking the spine, he laughed when he read the title: Moby Dick.

Was it a leaky tuna sandwich innocently permeating the book, or was it a prank? School pranks have a long history. Some are harmless, but most exact some degree of pain or embarrassment. Although we can't eliminate pranks, we can lessen their frequency by creating around us an atmosphere of acceptance, trust, and respect. If we can exemplify these values and show our students that diversity is a blessing, then we can enjoy some good, clean fun.

**God, may we enjoy laughter in the classroom, but not at the expense of anyone's feelings.**

*A*fter fifteen years of teaching and continuing education, the new principal came down to breakfast wearing her new suit, excited about the coming day.

Her husband, who was reading the morning paper, groaned, "Sit down, dear. I think you'd better hear this."

"Let me get my cereal first," she chirped.

"No," he said. "You'll get indigestion. Listen to your announcement in the news."

It read: "After an extensive search, no well-qualified candidate was found to fill the principal's post at Riverview. After a closed session on Monday, the school board is honored to announce the appointment of Dr. Ann Good to the position."

Can one wrong word burst your bubble?

Don't allow a misprint, a jealous comment, or an ignorant remark to dampen your spirits. Remember, nothing less than hard work and dedication brings you the fulfillment of a goal; it is something you do for your own edification and for the glory of God. Whatever praise or criticism others offer is secondary. Give thanks today for the talents God has given you.

> **May I always praise you, Great Giver, through my achievements and rejoice with you over the goodness of my life.**

*T*he teacher took note of a student who was hunched over her desk and shielding her face with a notebook. During his lecture, he came close enough to see that she was crying silently.

After class, he asked, "What's the matter, Keisha?"

"My parents won't listen to me!" she sobbed, and she proceeded to tell her tale of woe.

"It sounds like they listened to you," commented the teacher, "but you don't want to hear what they're saying."

Teachers, of all people, expect to be listened to and heard; but do we ever ask ourselves if we are good listeners?

When we have a critique, do we grow defensive and close our ears? As we sit with a parent, are we rehearsing what we're going to say instead of hearing the concern? In the teacher's lounge, do we talk too much about ourselves when someone else needs an ear?

Let those who have ears listen, because God speaks to us through parents and friends, coworkers and students, guiding us toward the greater good.

**Through prayer, O God, may I turn down the noise in my head so that I can listen to others.**

*O*ne Wednesday, the four-year-olds' class could not share, would not cooperate, and had no patience with themselves or anyone else. The preschool teacher felt like she spent all day drying tears of hurt, disappointment, and frustration. "How was school today, Mrs. Latta?" asked a cheerful father.

"Oh, we had a bawl," she sighed.

Sometimes we're filled with frustration over our coworkers, the bureaucracy, the kids, or ourselves. The pressure builds inside us and, just as when we were little, we need to let it out. Shouting, swearing, or being sarcastic is rarely as therapeutic as a good cry.

The book of Ecclesiastes states that there is a "time to weep," which is different from "a time to break down . . . mourn . . . [or] lose" (3:3-6). As adults, let's give ourselves the time, the space, and the permission to weep.

> **Be my comfort, Lord, so the tears can fall when they need to.**

*T*he school had a student court, and a defendant who was charged with many misdeeds was sentenced by a jury of his peers. Some of his buddies who were waiting in the hall said, "Don't tell us what you did; just tell us what they're going to do to you."

Our society says that it values *justice*, but it seems to focus primarily on *judgment* instead. The popularity of real courtroom cases on television proves the point.

There's something about human nature that inclines us to interest ourselves in other people's business and make judgments about them. Knowing our mortal weakness, Jesus said, "With the judgment you make you will be judged, and the measure you give will be the measure you get" (Matthew 7:2).

When we are tempted to busy ourselves with negative talk, let's remember that judgment also awaits us.

**Forgive me, Merciful One, for the many times I have lacked understanding, tolerance, or mercy for others.**

*E*very Friday the parochial school invited a guest to come and speak about his or her faith. Usually Mary was so anxious about preparing her lessons that she would skip the program to work in her classroom. One day a colleague called to her, "Martha! Please come with me to the assembly today."

"Why did you call me 'Martha'?" Mary asked.

"You're acting more like a 'Martha,' but if you come with me, I'll call you Mary again."

In Luke's story of Martha and Mary (Luke 10:38-42), Martha gets a bit grumpy because she is slaving away in the kitchen while Mary sits at Jesus' feet receiving spiritual nourishment. When Martha protests the situation, Jesus tells her that "Mary has chosen the better part, which will not be taken away from her" (v. 42).

Like our education, our spiritual enlightenment cannot be taken away from us. Every day we need to spend some time at the feet of Jesus. Despite demands and distractions, we have need of this "better part."

> **When I am anxious about many things, remind me, Lord, that I can come to you.**

*T*he middle-schooler muttered "I hate math!" as she dragged into the classroom.

"Why so negative?" responded the pre-algebra teacher.

"Because I'm the worst at math," she stated flatly.

"In this class, I'll help you turn a negative into a positive," beamed the teacher.

"Is that some kind of algebra joke?" she said with a hint of a smile.

Every year in our classes there are students who have a difficult time with the subject or subjects we teach. They may suffer from a developmental lag, a learning disability, or a previous bad experience. These students need a reason to try. They won't be tempted by "academic challenge" or the notion that they'll need to know this material someday. But they might do it to please *us*.

Let's give our students a reason to like us and work with us, especially if they don't like our subject.

> **Understanding God, sometimes I don't like the lesson I have to learn, but I'm thankful that your love sees me through.**

*O* *ne boy began staying inside during recess to clean the classroom.*

*"Sam, why aren't you outside playing with your friends?" queried his teacher.*

*"Because this room gets so messy!" he answered as he plucked trash from the floor.*

*"Why does that concern you?" she asked.*

*"Well, if my mom can't keep up with the mess three kids make, how can the custodian keep up with three hundred kids?"*

Teresa of Avila said, "Our Lord does not care so much for the importance of our works as for the love in which they are done." Young children seem to know this. Never doubting their expressions of love, they believe their works will make a real difference.

Adults, and even older children, can become jaded, discounting the importance of small acts of kindness. Each of us, young and old, can share our love in little ways every day. It *will* make a difference.

> **God of Love, may I come to understand that love only grows when it is shared.**

*T*he student teacher worked diligently in hopes of creating a wonderful language arts unit for her kindergartners. At first, the children were impressed with the myriad activities; but after a few days, they were as exhausted as their teacher.

*Noticing her drooping students, she asked, "What's wrong? What can I do?"*

*"All we want," said one little girl, "is for you to read us a story."*

Sometimes in our desire to expand or improve upon an idea, we just succeed in complicating it. When things get complicated, we become stressed.

Eventually, whether in our lives or in our lesson plans, we have an epiphany: simplify! When we choose simplicity, we can pare away the extraneous and discover what is essential in our work, in our relationships, and in our faith. Realizing what is essential to our health and happiness will keep us uncomplicated and on course. Simplicity is beautiful!

---

**Eternal One, help me to keep things simple whenever I can.**

---

*L* *aura did not want to play her clarinet in the evening band concert. She was upset with her band teacher and was refusing to perform. When her parents insisted that she participate, Laura retorted, "You can make me go tonight, but you can't make me play a single note!"*

There are times when we, like Laura, are simply going through the motions. When we are present in body but not in spirit, perhaps it is time for a change. Occasionally, the path to change is clear, but most of the time we aren't certain which way to turn. What change do we need? How will we find it? Will it work out?

Jesus advises us: "Ask, and it will be given you; search, and you will find; knock, and the door will be opened for you" (Matthew 7:7). Turn to God. Pray daily to move in a better direction, either within yourself or within a situation. Trust the Lord to open a door.

**When I am unfulfilled and disappointed, God, please guide me toward an open door.**

*A* s the class studied the parts of a worship
service, the Sunday school teacher illustrated
the lesson with photographs. He quizzed the
students about each photo, ranging from the choir
processing to the minister offering the benediction.
The presentation ended with a photo of a baby held
near a baptismal font.

"Tell me about this photo," he requested.

"It's a baby being sanitized!" proclaimed one little
girl.

Don't we sometimes wish that our students could
be "sanitized"? In the younger grades we deal with
runny noses, vomit, head lice, bathroom accidents,
cuts and scrapes, and loose teeth on a regular basis.
In the older grades we are faced with the changes of
puberty, poor personal hygiene habits, and a variety
of injuries and illnesses. On a particularly bad day, we
think, "I'm a teacher; why do I have to do this?"; but
we understand it's part of the job to care for their
"health" as well as their minds.

As a teacher, Jesus tended to the physical woes of
his followers even as he taught them. So, when you
are in the middle of a gross or unpleasant situation,
remember that Jesus can sympathize.

> **Lord, help me to be a comforter when my
> students have physical needs.**

*T*he pregnant drama teacher, determined to see the cast through dress rehearsals, was surprised when her water broke at the last bell. "I can make it a few more hours," she said confidently to a parent volunteer.

Her labor began anyway, but she continued to call out stage directions and coach her thespians. Suddenly, she was gripped by an extraordinary pain. The parent helped her to the floor of the darkened auditorium as the show went on.

Soon the teacher's moans and groans broke through the onstage drama, and the cast fell silent. Awestruck and blinded by the stage lights, the students waited while their teacher became a mother. When the infant's cries rang out, someone said, "That baby sure knows how to make an entrance!"

The birth of a baby is a real showstopper; and for anyone who has witnessed the experience, it is a miracle. Despite the wondrous nature of the event, we nevertheless expect to see or hear of this particular miracle again. Yet we are rarely so expectant of other miracles coming into our lives. Do we recognize and appreciate the "luck," "coincidence," or "twists of fate" in our lives as everyday miracles?

Maybe it's time we learned to expect a miracle.

**Thank you, God, for all the miracles in my life.**

*O*n a hot spring afternoon, the director of the parochial preschool saw on the playground a girl who was licking her arm.

*"What are you doing?" asked the director.*

*"I'm tasting myself," replied the child.*

*"Why?" the director asked.*

*"My teacher told me I was the salt of the earth— and she was right!"*

Has there ever been a time in your life when you held back your opinions, your temper, your enthusiasm, or your ideas until you became a bland version of your former self? Regardless of your reasons, it didn't feel right to be a lukewarm person. Jesus speaks to this in Matthew 5:13. He says that we are salt, but that if we lose our saltiness, we become worthless. Similarly, in Revelation 3:15-16, he says that it is better to be hot or cold than an unpalatable "lukewarm."

As we approach our teaching, our friendships, and our faith, may we remember that it is better to have salt in ourselves than to be bland but "safe" people.

> **Glorious God, give me the courage not to hold back when I should step forward.**

*C*andy, a seventh-grader, had quite a reputation *for silly questions and spacey behavior, although she was constantly on the honor roll. When her health class met on Friday, the teacher randomly assigned each student to write a report on a particular organ of the body. The reports were due on Monday.*

*Monday arrived, and Candy volunteered to present her report first.*

*As she held her macaroni model, she said, "I am the brain; it is my job to think." After a momentary pause, Candy made eye contact with the class, and everyone burst into laughter.*

Howard Gardner, a professor at Harvard University, has identified eight "frames of reference" or kinds of intelligence that people possess: visual/spatial, naturalistic, kinesthetic, reflective, musical, linguistic, interpersonal, and logical-mathematical. We are coming to understand that intelligence is not something we can measure in one way only.

God has given us differing gifts of aptitude in varying combinations to create our intelligence. It's time to appreciate and celebrate the mystery of the brain!

> **Lord, help me to teach in a way that brings out the best in each person.**

*F* *altering attendance in the teen Sunday school*
*class motivated a new pair of teachers to lead*
*the group. They planned interactive and cre-*
*ative lessons, debriefed each other after each class to*
*make improvements, sent cool postcards to the kids,*
*and brought a delicious treat for the class every*
*Sunday.*

*Pleased with the growing attendance, one teacher*
*pulled a student aside, asking, "Do you think the*
*class is going better?"*

*"Well," he replied, "the food really helps."*

Kids are always hungry, and their interest in class
is often increased by the presence of an occasional
snack. There are those who question the appropriate-
ness of food in the classroom, and there are others
who appreciate the improvement of attitudes and
attendance. In any case, food is a blessing, and there
is a joy in sharing it.

When the apostle Paul addressed early Christians
who were concerned about what they ate and with
whom, he encouraged them to eat and be thankful,
saying, "So, whether you eat or drink, or whatever
you do, do everything for the glory of God" (1 Corinthians 10:31). If we choose to offer a treat along
with a lesson, may we do both to God's glory.

---

**Bounteous Lord, thank you for the
pleasure of sharing food with your children.**

*A* class from a parochial school went on a field trip to Washington, D.C. While they were on the subway, there was a power failure and the lights went out. The children were frightened; so to calm them, their teacher thought of a Bible verse with light imagery. "Children, let's say the verse 'Your Word is a lamp to my feet,' " she encouraged.

*After a few minutes of the children's chanting, the lights popped on.*

*"God sure keeps his word!" a boy said earnestly.*

If we want children to know that God's Word is a lamp, shining in the darkness, then we must light that lamp. When we read from the Bible, quote a verse in conversation, pray, or share a spiritual experience, we give them a spark of faith.

While some of us should take care to separate church and state when at school, we still can behave as people of God, kindling awareness and belief.

**May I help others find a path to you, Lord.**

*A* t the school's fall festival, there were many booths offering games, face painting, and food. An altercation at the chili dog stand brought a teacher to investigate. *"What's the problem?" she asked.*

*"That boy Max is hanging around smelling the chili dogs," grumbled the seller. "He's annoying, and he's ruining our business."*

*"Hum," the teacher pondered. "Max, do you have any money?"*

*"Yeah," Max replied, jingling the change in his pocket.*

*"Did you hear that?" the teacher inquired of the seller.*

*"Yes, but—"*

*"Consider yourself paid!" she said to the seller. And to Max she said, "Take your business elsewhere!"*

Teachers are relied upon to settle arguments, break up fights, and initiate peace talks between the warring camps in the classroom. It's not easy, but it is necessary if any learning is to continue.

If such duties are not recognized in your contract and you're not receiving "battle compensation," don't despair. Your reward will come someday. "Blessed are the peacemakers, for they will be called children of God" (Matthew 5:9).

---

**Be with me, Lord, as I settle disputes and work to maintain peace.**

*I*t had been quite a day for fund-raisers. Ms. Hilou began by pledging to her public radio station. Next she contributed to the Friends of the Library, and then she purchased popcorn and oranges from the local Boy Scout troop. At 6:00 P.M. she arrived at a downtown shopping district where the stores were donating profits to her son's school for the next hour. Thirty minutes later she deposited about $100 worth of merchandise at the register and searched her purse for a credit card as a school volunteer rang up the sale.

*Just moments after scanning the card, the volunteer whispered, "You're over your credit limit, Ma'am."*

*"I have definitely reached my limit!" snapped Ms. Hilou, turning on her heels.*

*"Wait! I made a mistake!" apologized the cashier. "Your total is $101, not $10,100!"*

Everywhere we turn it seems that someone is seeking our financial support. We know that God has blessed us with much, but how should we respond to all these solicitations? The Bible says: "Each of you must give as you have made up your mind, not reluctantly or under compulsion, for God loves a cheerful giver" (2 Corinthians 9:7). Therefore, we should choose the causes that hold personal meaning—ones that we can support with our hearts and our hands, as well as our money.

**God of Abundance, with thanks for all
I have received, I will share with others.**

*D*uring social studies class, everyone was telling about an occupation they found interesting. When Juan's turn came, he reported, "Both my parents are doctors. They took the hypocrite's oath!"

The young, full of unquestioning belief in all the rules, values, and morals they've been taught, have a keen radar for adult hypocrisy. They manage to catch us every time we do not practice what we preach, and they accept no excuses.

Jesus, who thoroughly understood the ways of the world, was similarly impatient with hypocrites. He was especially angry with hypocritical leaders who were charged with teaching morality and setting an example. Because we are teachers, we also are held to a higher standard. While this may feel burdensome, it can be an incentive to live as honestly and with as much integrity as possible.

**Almighty God, may I be worthy of the trust and respect that is given to me as a teacher.**

*M*r. Moreno's chemistry course always began with a safety lecture, which he had repeated for the past twenty years. The students, who were seated at lab tables, listened halfheartedly to his monotone speech.

"... Do not play with matches, or they will hurt you. Do not spill anything, or it will hurt you. Do not put anything in the electrical outlets or ...," he droned.

At that very moment, Harry was absently poking a foil gum wrapper at the socket in front of him. Suddenly a bright blue flash propelled him backward. As he crashed to the floor, Harry choked, "Or it will hurt you!"

Consequences can be a real shock to some students. Fortunately, school is a great place for children to learn about consequences—that is, if we have the diligence required to carry them out. Proverbs 13:24 says: "Those who spare the rod hate their children, but those who love them are diligent to discipline them." These days we do not apply the rod, but may we have the love to teach our children about consequences.

**Disciplining is not an easy task. God, help me to be fair, timely, and consistent with my students.**

*T*he football players had been relentless in their teasing of the cheerleaders. The girls were greatly offended and determined to teach the team a lesson.

*Playing into the boys' sexist perceptions, the cheerleaders brought the players an enormous batch of homemade brownies—laced with a chocolate laxative.*

*"About time you future homemakers brought us a snack," jested a lineman.*

*"Oh, we're delighted to share our latest recipe," cooed a coed.*

*"Mmm," muttered a senior behind her pom-poms, "a recipe for disaster."*

In a few hours the cheerleaders had turned a bunch of hecklers into a horde of enemies, creating a messy situation. Disastrous situations also can arise among the faculty or the administration. Unfortunately, when politics or rivalries are allowed to fester, colleagues can become enemies.

In the Old Testament days, there was an "eye for an eye" policy toward enemies; but with the ministry of Jesus came a new covenant: to love our enemies. Difficult? Yes. Impossible? No, for with "faith the size of a mustard seed . . . nothing will be impossible for you" (Matthew 17:20).

**Loving Lord, grant me the strength to resist hatred, and the power to generate love.**

*M*r. Moses, you've had such an outstanding year teaching first grade, why do you wish to transfer to the fourth grade?" inquired the principal.

"Separation anxiety," quipped the teacher.

*He went on to explain: "My twins will be first-graders next year, and if I don't have some separation between the children at home and the children at school, I'll go crazy!"*

It's challenging to be a good teacher all day and then come home ready to be a good parent. After a long day, we may have a rather short attention span, with a short temper to match. The children we love most dearly become targets for our tension, if we're not careful.

The Bible advises us not to provoke our children or they may lose heart (Colossians 3:21). So, before we take our stress out on our families, let's find a few minutes to walk, pray, dance, meditate, play the piano, or shoot some hoops. Establishing a little separation between work and home will create a lot less anxiety.

> **Help me to recharge and refresh, Lord, so that I may be the kind of parent my children are eager to see.**

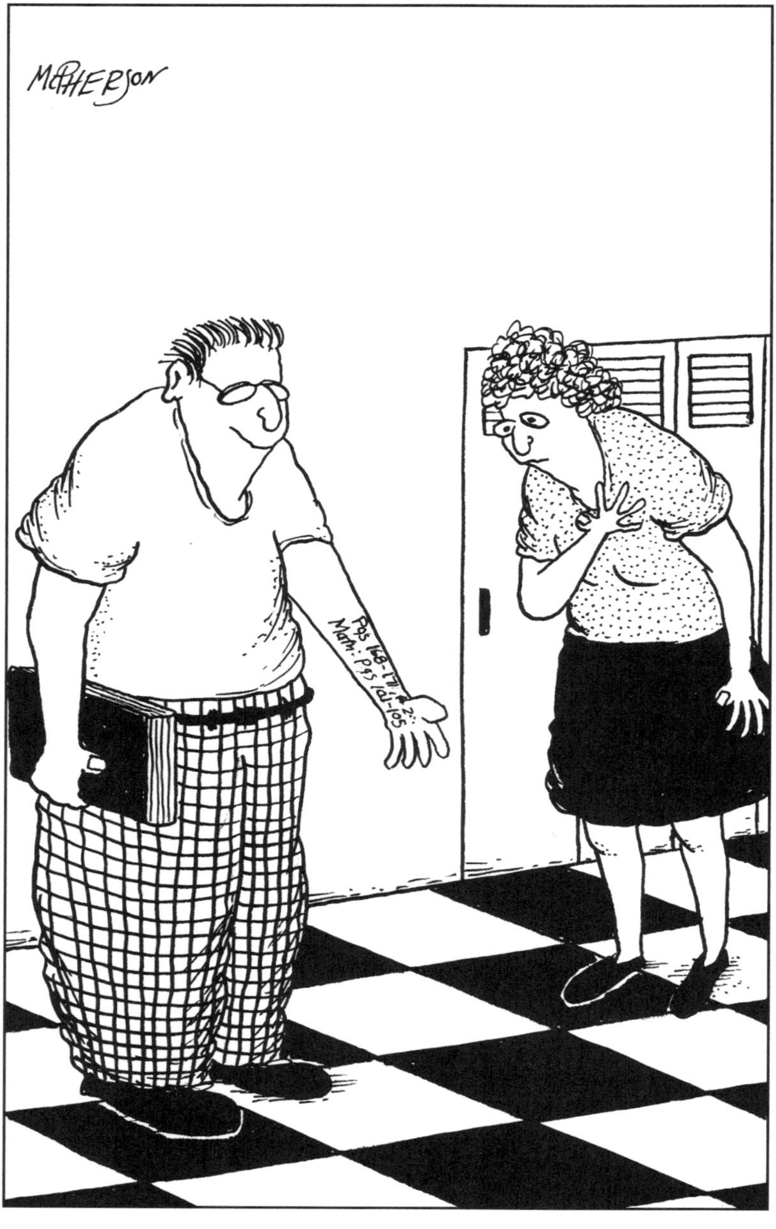
McPHERSON
Pgs 168-171 #2;
Math: Pgs 101-105

*A* teacher stopped a student in the hallway, demanding, "Show me what's written on your arm!"

*Obediently, the student extended a forearm, which was covered in writing from a felt-tip pen.*

*Grasping the boy's arm, the teacher exclaimed, "This looks terrible!"*

*"Yeah, those are all my assignments," explained the boy. "I've got homework up to my elbow!"*

Every teacher has to make a decision regarding homework: how much, how often, and how will it count toward a final grade? Some of us hate homework as much as the students, because we have to grade it all. Others of us appear to take "school" home with us every day. When considering the issue, our responsibility is to find a balance—not only for our students' sake, but also for our own. God wishes us to have balance between work and rest, so that we may value both.

**As I assign homework, O God, help me to do what is most beneficial for my students.**

*F*or Vacation Bible School, members of a congregation participated in a Bible times marketplace. Adults and children, dressed in costume, were making bricks, weaving baskets, selling fruit, fashioning leather pouches, and creating pottery. Near the front of the church, a teacher was tending some sheep and a flock of children.

Seeing a letter carrier approach, he called, "Ho, messenger! What news have you?"

As if she had been waiting for such an occasion, she addressed the shepherds, "I am bringing you good news of great joy for all the people: to you is born this day in the city of David a Savior, who is the Messiah, the Lord" (Luke 2:10-11).

Then, handing over the mail, she added, "I'm no angel of the Lord, but I have taught Sunday school for twelve years."

Sunday school teachers are perennial students of the Word. Reading Scripture, studying Bible background, and pondering the spiritual message are cornerstones of each lesson. As we teach lesson after lesson, it's not surprising that we grow in faith as well as in our understanding of the Bible. By sharing our faith, we build it up; by teaching others, we learn so much.

---

**I praise you, Lord, for the blessings of your Word.**

---

*M*any children have summer birthdays. No school during the summer means that their names are never read during announcements, their parents never deliver cupcakes or pizza, and the schoolfriends the students would celebrate with may be on vacation.

*Knowing this, Ms. Shanklin informed her class that she would host a summer birthday celebration on the last day of school. Not comprehending the teacher, a worried little girl said, "I'll be almost six on Friday; can I come?"*

Most children have a fresh, unself-conscious joy in celebrating their birthdays. They freely accept the love and affection offered them and radiate the happiness they feel.

Through baptism, the birthday of our faith, we become eternal children of God. We, too, should celebrate our spiritual growth by joyfully accepting God's love. When we truly allow that holy love to abide in us, we reflect a happiness that lights up the world around us.

> **God, when I celebrate the birthdays of others, help me to remember to rejoice in my birth in Jesus Christ.**

*Zach had a difficult time staying awake in history class. After several admonitions by his teacher, Mr. Wong, he had an idea. After making a steeple with his fingers, he rested his forehead atop them. As the room grew warm and the lecture grew long, sleep overtook him.*

*Still lecturing, Mr. Wong approached Zach's desk and rapped on it sharply. As his head snapped up, Zach shouted, "Amen!"*

*"What were you doing?" Mr. Wong demanded.*

*"Praying, sir," replied Zach.*

*"I guess you were praying for after-school detention, because you just got it," Mr. Wong replied.*

We are accustomed to admonishing our students, but what do we do when a fellow teacher is acting too flirtatious, flying into a rage with a student, or telling inappropriate jokes in class? Despite our discomfort, we may believe that it is necessary to address our peer. Perhaps the Scriptures can guide us: "Bear with one another . . . forgive each other. . . . Clothe yourselves with love. . . . Let the word of Christ dwell in you richly; teach and admonish one another in all wisdom. . . . And whatever you do, in word or deed, do everything in the name of the Lord" (Colossians 3:13-17).

---

**I pray for your guidance, Lord, when I need to express my concern to a colleague.**

---

*C*arlos came running to his teacher as she
entered the classroom.
*"Teddy is missing!" he sobbed.*

*A quick check of the cage revealed that the guinea
pig was gone. So the teacher and the student began a
crawling search for the pet. When Teddy was finally
located among the dress-up clothes, the child was
relieved but not completely happy.*

*"Is anything else the matter?" asked the teacher.*

*"Well, I got Teddy out of his cage and he ran
away," Carlos confessed. "I told the wrong truth."*

We say that we want the truth and that we value
the truth; but when we must tell the truth, it's not so
easy! Even though we're adults, we sometimes tell the
"wrong truth" because we can't admit our mistakes
and sins. This problem must be as old as the Bible,
for the Word says, "If we say that we have no sin, we
deceive ourselves, and the truth is not in us" (1 John
1:8). When the truth is not in us, we cannot be happy
or at peace. Confessing our wrongdoing to God allows
us to cast off deception and live in truth.

**God of Mercy, help me to recognize my errors
so that I may confess them to you.**

*T*hree sixth-grade girls were smitten with their handsome science teacher, and they were determined to see him as often as possible. Their investigations revealed that he liked to volunteer. So, in September, they volunteered to do a river cleanup because he was the crew chief. Learning that he bagged groceries at the food bank every other Friday, they signed up to help too. When he participated in a charity 5K run, they were there dispensing water.

"Goodness, you girls do a lot of volunteer work!" he exclaimed. "I see you everywhere I go!"

"You're our inspiration," they sighed.

Although he was the girls' motivation for volunteering, the teacher's real inspiration was his faith. He agreed with the passage from James which says, "Show me your faith apart from your works, and I by my works will show you my faith" (James 2:18).

Our faith has both an inward and outward expression. Through our outward service to others, we fulfill Jesus' command to love our neighbors as ourselves. We also may set an example for the young who are watching us.

---

**Lord, may I demonstrate my faith in you by being your hands in the world.**

---

*I*n the waning afternoon light, the history teacher graded the essay questions covering the internment of the Japanese during World War II. Although students regularly mangled his beloved subject, he had never grown accustomed to it. On this day, however, one student received credit for an essay. Despite the errors, the words conveyed a meaning, as the teacher grudgingly acknowledged. It read: "During the second Weird War, the Japanese were sent to interim camps. The U.S. ceased their homes and belongings. These people felt scarred when they were sent away."

Thoughts are the genesis of words, and words are powerful. They can be used to hurt or heal; imprison or liberate; influence a student or a society.

The very young believe that we, their teachers, are always right. And the older students, who may not appear to be listening, are more attentive than we imagine. We have a responsibility to choose our words carefully, for our words carry the weight of authority.

> **In the beginning was the Word, and the Word was you, God. I humbly ask that you guide my words as I work with your children.**

*O*n the previous Sunday, Mrs. Ely's class had broken ground for a garden. As they pulled weeds and rocks from the rich soil, she told the class the parable of the sower. The following Sunday, the children brought in seeds to plant. By turns, the children eagerly showed their packets to Mrs. Ely, who started each one on a row. Finally, she came to a child holding a box.

"What kind of seed do you have, Beth?" she asked.

"Birdseed!" she announced proudly.

Anytime we teach we hope and pray that the seeds of knowledge find fertile ground, taking root in our students. That is especially true when we teach the Word of God's kingdom. The roots of early faith can sustain us into adulthood, drawing us back to church and helping us flourish spiritually. Those of us who spent our childhoods in wonderful Sunday school classes were blessed. All thanks to the teachers who sang, crafted, told stories, organized plays, and planted gardens with us.

> **God of Life, may I grow in faith where I am planted.**

*M*onday through Friday she is a teacher at a private school, but when the weekend arrives, she becomes the Queen of Bargains. *One Saturday, she was browsing her favorite thrift shop when she was spotted by a parent.*

*"Hello, dear. I see you've brought in an armful of donations, too," said the matron.*

*The teacher replied, "Oh no, Mrs. Potts. I'm buying my new spring wardrobe!"*

None of us went into teaching with the idea of becoming wealthy. Our reasons for choosing to teach are not based on material aspirations; however, we live in a society that encourages us to want the latest and greatest. Lest we get caught up in the values of a materialistic culture, we must remember that money cannot buy happiness. Pleasure, which appeals to the body, is fleeting; but true happiness, which is born of the Spirit, can be ours regardless of our financial status.

> **May I find joy in what I have, O God,
> rather than having to find joy.**

*T*he spry, white-haired teacher took his students on a trip to the woods as part of a unit on ecology. They learned about seedlings and saplings, the canopy and the understory, nurse logs and parasites. They found birds' nests, deer tracks, and the stump of a giant old tree. Together they counted its rings.

*"It looks like one hundred seventy-six," the teacher announced.*

*"Was that tree as old as you?" asked a child as she patted his wrinkled hand.*

Our earth is so ancient that it is difficult to comprehend the number of seasons it took to create the mountains, rivers, and great forests. Even an oak tree has a life span longer than ours. Yet, within that oak tree's life, our culture has had an impact on the environment. As we lead our students through the woods or through a unit of study on ecology, let's engender in them a sense of wonder and a sense of responsibility for God's creation. May we be good stewards of this priceless trust.

> **God of Heaven and Earth, help me to see beyond my day or my life to understand how I can work to protect your creation.**

*E*very week since school began, Ms. Shoemaker's boyfriend sent her a bouquet of flowers for her desk. The students found this, and other tokens of endearment, to be very exciting. One day, just before the class went to lunch, the teacher's boyfriend popped in unexpectedly. On bended knee, he clasped her hand, saying, "Katy, will you marry me?" Before she could reply, a girl jumped from her desk, shouting, "She will! She will!"

In these days, when students are continually warned about their interactions with the opposite sex, it's delightful for everyone to see a sweet, wholesome romance followed by the covenant of marriage. Knowledge about sexual harassment, date rape, AIDS, and sexually transmitted diseases may be necessary in today's world, but it also is quite valuable for kids to see that committed love exists and that the sacrament of marriage is blessed by God.

> **Lord, I pray that my students will not be hurt by the negative side of sexuality and will respect the gift of love they have to offer.**

*S* *ubstitute teachers were complaining about the children in Ms. Pipkin's class. Concerned, Ms. Pipkin decided to bring an end to the problem by putting on a little masquerade.*

*The next day she dressed in costume, effecting the look of a senior citizen, complete with cane and hearing aid. With a wink to her colleagues, she entered her own classroom as a substitute. Before long, she overheard two students talking.*

*"It's gonna be hard to act mean to a little old lady," complained one.*

*"Yeah, but we've got to," argued the other. "How else can we keep Ms. Pipkin from leaving?"*

Do we ever really like a substitute for anything? After all, it's not what we want or expect; it's simply second best. The students loved their teacher; and when she wasn't there, they missed the security, happiness, and sense of purpose she gave them.

Sometimes we feel like we're missing the security, happiness, or sense of purpose we want in our lives. At those times there's no substitute for faith. Through our faith, we are meant to become the persons God created us to be, not second best but beloved.

> **Help me to fulfill my inner purpose, Lord,
> and thereby find contentment.**